D1053211

Arranged and Introduced by PHILIP KOPPER

With Masterworks Selected by Mary Carll Kopper

stmas

ment

Stewart, Tabori & Chang,
Publishers, Inc., New York

Design and calligraphic headings
by WEI-WEN CHANG

Text calligraphy by
POLLY JOHNSON

Library of Congress Cataloging in Publication Data
Kopper, Philip
A Christmas testament
1. Christmas. I. Title
BV45.K78 1982 232.9'21 82-5843
ISBN 0-941434-23-0 AACR2

Published in 1982 by Stewart, Tabori & Chang, Publishers, Inc., New York.

Distributed by Workman Publishing
708 Broadway
New York, New York 10003

Printed in Japan.

FOR GRACE

AND

ALL HER PEOPLE

Contents

Foreword

This book was written for everyone who celebrates Christmas, and in the English-speaking world that means almost everybody: devout and barely nominal Christians of every denomination, Liberal Jews augmenting their older Festival of Lights, avowed agnostics, even affirmed athiests who practice the ritual of presents. Not the product of strict, original scholarship, nor a work of any doctrinal orthodoxy, *A Christmas Testament* grew out of a small labor of love. Originally it was a sort of gift to a small community of friends.

Several years ago the young rector of a century-old church asked me to prepare a new Christmas program. Our congregation had often used a service arranged by an Archbishop for an English cathedral then altered and performed at King's College, Cambridge, for two generations. Plainly called "Lessons and Carols," it offered a medley of songs and ancient texts from the King James Bible, the poetic exemplar since 1611. The readings included familiar passages from the Gospels, notably accounts of the Nativity from St.Matthew and St.Luke, along with Old Testament verses that, according to concensus, prefigured the coming of Christ. By tradition, nine readers would take the pulpit in order of age, from the youngest child capable of addressing the congregation to the oldest communicant who could make himself heard. After each lesson came a carol.

For fifteen hundred years, ever since the first celebration of Jesus' birth, Christmas practices have been remarkably flexible. With that tradition in mind, I adapted the English service, added some passages, deleted others, and arranged the texts into a single narrative. Uninterrupted by music, it became a voice play that opened with words from Genesis in the chalice-shaking basso of a stout, old man who had heard tales at Robert Louis Stevenson's knee and stamped his cane for emphasis. It continued with the pronouncement of prophesy through a mouthful of braces by a little girl in pigtails. One lawyer played Herod and another the Angel Gabriel. The cast included a bureaucrat, the student who became my wife (and artful collaborator here), an English diplomat's wife, and the Alabama-born minister. Their accents combined in an aural pageant of awe and joy.

These pages resurrect that service in a palpable and visual form. Although it relates Matthew's and Luke's accounts in the King James cadences, it is not Gospel verbatim. It includes modern punctuation and omits some old words that acquired new or clashing meanings. In one instance, *A Christmas Testament* follows a librettist's phrasing that Handel immortalized in the *Messiah*. Extraneous passages within the texts have been deleted (and for the sake of graphic clarity these are not indicated by ellipses). Yet this version contains the New Testament Nativity passages in almost all their surprisingly short entirety along with parts of related episodes, such as Zacharias' declaration of the Magnificat. In other words, it tells the story we have inherited, a remarkably short story as it happens, for one overlooked miracle of Christmas lies in the brevity of its sources: Parts of four chapters in two Biblical books—no more than fifteen hundred words—inspired all the many rites and trappings of Christmas around the world. This uniquely universal holiday—garish and glorious, symbolic and physical, secular and sacred—blossomed in astonishing variety from tiny literary seeds in the New Testament.

Yet to use only New Testament texts, let alone the Nativity passages per se, robs the story of its extraordinarily powerful context. It's hard to find a satisfying place to start in the Gospels, which so often evoke earlier passages. For example, Luke's first mention of Mary begins, "And in the sixth month...." Of what? Of her cousin Elisabeth's confinement before bearing John the Baptist. That birth was almost as miraculous as Christ's and was foretold by prophets who had been speaking of a Messiah for ages. Prophesies and angelic messengers harken all the way back to God's covenant with Abraham, itself a sequel to Adam and Eve's fall. Thus the search for the story's beginning leads back to Eden and before.

Because I love the story itself, I tried to compose a cogent reading version—for our time—of the timeless tale. The music in it echoes the antique words and meters. The meanings, magic, and miracles reflect in the beholder's eye. Read as divine revelation or deathless myth, here is an account of ancient heroics and villainy, of honor and doubt, obedience and daring, rage and serenity, of human perplexity, simple beauty, and inexplicable mystery. It is as old as Isaiah, as new as this edition. This story, told in many tongues throughout many generations, still speaks to humankind—and shall again. Amen.

12 thoughts

# of christmas

1 As the end of every year draws near, the northern days' light wanes in the looming face of winter. Then the solstice saves the sun again; and before the days even seem to lengthen, Christmas comes. Holy night and holiday, sacred and secular, symbolic as dreams and real as a drumstick, it brightens our world in a galaxy of ways.

The centerpiece of winter, this day has brought brief armistice between warring armies. By modern tradition, it is the day when scattered families gather together. For generations it has been the single occasion when all give gifts and receive them too.

Christmas was not ever thus, but it evolved this way. It is a manifold miracle.

2 In Europe and the Americas, almost everybody celebrates Christmas. Doctrinaire celebrants insist that all importance lies in just one miracle: the ancient birth in Bethlehem. I won't deny that belief or debate such a weighty matter, but I do suggest that two temporal matters match the theological one in miraculous degree.

First, this holiday is observed in every land on earth. A uniquely catholic occasion, it is celebrated by devout sectarians and nonbelievers, by public multitudes and cabals in secret cells. People celebrate in ways as contrary as mindless revelry and out-of-mind meditation, as dissonant as Gregorian chant and "Jingle Bell Rock."

Second, the brief and epic tale found in Gospel fragments has come to involve an extraordinary spectrum of traditions. Some seem to relate directly to Biblical events, as gift-giving may recall the Magi. Other particulars like Mexican piñatas, Dickensian feasts, and German evergreens arose from alien origins to be embraced within the boundless repertoire of Christmas.

Here lies the miracle too often overlooked: Not only did Christmas come to reach around the world, it adopted customs from every people it encountered. Thus in every region its pagan and parochial elements became so tightly woven as to seem essential strands of a single fabric.

3 People everywhere have always adapted the simple saga to suit themselves. Fra Angelico clad his Virgins in flowing finery, the "modern dress" of his day. Flemish painters saw Bethlehem in snowy lowland settings. African madonnas have ebony skin. In Eastern legend, a date palm bent its boughs so Mary could eat; the tale was transplanted and transformed in Europe where it took root as a cherry tree that bowed its branches to offer more familiar fruit.

Our Christmas celebrations combine Aramaic episode and Roman rite, Druid decoration and German fir, a Dutch saint's bounty and astronomical accident, Hebrew prophesy and Greek hearsay. Yet its core lies in four-score verses of the Bible. How easily we forget that simple fact amid the neon and the dogma, the glitter and the carols.

Think of the living disparities: stockings hung by false-front hearths that never held a fire; church doors standing brightly open this one cold midnight of the year; jewelers' windows sparkling with diamonds and plastic snow; a million turkeys roasting all at once; staid offices gone amok in mindless mirth; rainbows of ribbon candy and handmade kindergarten greetings; public charity and private prayer.

4 There's more mystery in Christmas trees than meets the eye. They came quietly to the New World with settlers early in the last century and then became a

national passion in the 1840s when a magazine pictured a model family gathered around one in their model home. That engraving in turn had been pirated from the *London Illustrated News*, which showed the royal family admiring their tree in Buckingham Palace. Prince Albert imported that one to honor a custom from his native Germany where Christmas trees supposedly arose. But history obscures their real origins.

Alsacian merchants sold them in the Strasbourg market as early as 1531, yet one historian of customs has found a written reference two decades before that—in Latvia. Other scholars hint at even earlier beginnings, whether or not trees were carried home and decorated in ancient halls. Every people in pre-Christian Europe revered trees in diverse ways. The Teutonic and Druidic words for *sanctuary* derive from the words for natural groves, glades, and woods.

As early as the fourteenth century, nominally Christian celebrations featured evergreens hung with apples to represent "the tree of life" on Adam and Eve's Day—December 24! The earliest link I can find between Christianity and trees of this kind dates from the eighth century when the missionary St. Boniface was abroad converting the Germans. He felled an oak sacred to Odin and then dedicated the little fir behind it to the Christ Child.

Like other delights of the season, the "traditional" Christmas tree may have little to do with the original nativity. But it has much to do with the complexities of Christmas as we have inherited it.

5 Santa Claus has a clear enough history. His name derives from the Dutch familiar form *Sinter Klaas* (for *Sint Nikolaas*), and he came to New Amsterdam with early colonists. In the Netherlands, St. Nicholas's Day brought a bearded man on a white horse into every town with presents for good children and coal for the bad. (Almost every country in Europe had a variation on this theme of the benevolent but just

visitor, who may harken all the way back to a terrible idol in ancient Mesopotamia.)

In 1822 Dr. Clement C. Moore, a New York theologian much respected for his scholarly *Commendious Lexicon of the Hebrew Language,* wrote a bedtime ditty called *A Visit From St. Nicholas* for his children. Passed on by a friend to a newspaper, the poem began "'Twas the night before Christmas," and it swept the land. Decades later, illustrator Thomas Nast pictured Moore's character much as we now imagine him.

Historically, Nicholas was a fourth-century Bishop of Asia Minor. Famous for good works, he was credited with many miracles, each so wonderful that he became a patron saint many times over as diverse groups of people—even nations such as Greece and Russia—claimed his special aegis. He reputedly calmed a storm at sea, and so sailors revered him as their own. He tossed three bags of gold into a pauper's house so that the poor man's daughters would have dowries. Thus Nicholas became the patron saint of both maidens and merchants. (The gold bags became the balls hanging outside pawnshops.) He revived three boys who had been drowned by a butcher in a barrel of brine and thus became the patron saint of children—and in time their special winter benefactor, indeed their "Santa Claus" at Christmas.

6 Over the centuries some Biblical events have been illustrated so often as to take on imagistic lives of their own, yet artists all but ignored others. Few masterpieces show Mary and Joseph arriving in Bethlehem or shepherds spreading the news. The world's museums contain a hundred stable scenes for every Flight into Egypt and a dozen of those for every return from that exile. Most painters worth remembering did at least one Annunciation and showed Mary hearing the Angel's word variously in awe, shock, or anger. But few painted the Angel visiting Joseph.

Manger scenes outnumber the rest, and artists placed mangers where their imaginations dictated, though a stable is never quite specified—only inferred from the text. According to one of the Gnostic gospels, which would be deemed heretical, the birth took place in a cave—a common enough place to tend and feed livestock—and some painters depicted that as the site of the manger. More often the birthplace is a building, whether hovel, brick barn, or anachronistic shrine with peacocks on the roof and trains of thousands following most splendid kings to pay the infant homage.

As a stable, the shelter became a focal point, a single symbol evoking the entire Nativity. Altered, embellished, elevated, the place that held the manger acquired its own inhabitants in mistaken fulfillment of a bogus prophesy. This was the result of an early translator's blunder in the Old Testament book of Habbakuk. As an English scholar explained the error, "Instead of 'in the midst of the years make (it) known,' we read 'Between two beasts Thou art made known.'" Although the error was later corrected, the ox and ass have benignly occupied the stable for sixteen centuries. Christmas would hardly seem the same without them. Custom has it that the animals warmed the babe with their breath and that beasts in barns speak at midnight each Christmas Eve. However familiar these figures seem, they are also addenda.

7 Theologians used to debate how many angels could fit on the head of a pin. Now scholars inquire how many authors put pen to parchment and composed holy writ. The Bible is a composite, an inspired collection echoing many voices and reflecting many points of view. One needn't read past its second chapter—as presently collated—to see the evidence.

In the first chapter of Genesis the creator, named simply God, made men and women in his image and gave them dominion over the earth. In the next chapter, eleven verses later, "the Lord God" made Adam alone out of dust and placed him in Eden to tend the garden where, in due time, He made woman from Adam's rib. This is a different account. At least two writers, harmonious but distinct, described the same event.

The book that starts "In the beginning" was not written first. Amos and Hosea, to name just two examples, appeared much earlier. But since the Creation must logically have occurred prior to all else, it came to open the Old Testament as books were added and their order rearranged.

Scholarship and science may one day deduce who crossed every "tau" in the New Testament and dotted every "shin" in the Old. But even the most detailed explication will fail to explain the Bible's impact completely. Written by many men and translated by others, it contains theology, history, folklore, law, poetry, biography, prophesy, and more. If it contains inconsistencies and contradictions, it nonetheless remains an extraordinary work—the most lasting composition of great meaning to people of many tongues through uncounted generations. Since the first recitation of the Twenty-third Psalm, it has possessed "the beauty of holiness." That might describe part of the Bible's truth but falls short of the whole, for this book also radiates the holiness of beauty.

8 Twenty-seven narratives became bound together as the New Testament, yet only two of its four Gospels describe the Nativity. Written relatively late, they differ from the rest of the sacred anthology and from each other in notable ways.

Luke, a physician and Paul's traveling companion, never knew Jesus man to man. The only Evangelist who wasn't a Jew, he wrote in belle-lettered Greek about A.D. 80 and traced Jesus' human ancestry all the way back to Adam, arguably for the benefit of his fellow gentiles. Matthew, a tax collector from Galilee, stressed the fulfillment of Old Testament prophesies in his account, which followed Jesus' genealogy only as far as the patriarch Abraham. He wrote in Aramaic, the lingua franca of Palestine, around the year 75 for a Jewish audience.

Both Matthew and Luke related parts of the story found

nowhere else. Matthew tells of Bethlehem's star and the Magi's trek. He relates Herod's expressed wish to worship the newborn child and then his spiteful treachery after he "saw he was mocked by the Wise Men" (or tricked, betrayed, or disobeyed) at the Angel's behest. Matthew also tells of the Innocents' slaughter and the flight into Egypt.

Neglecting those events, Luke's account includes Zacharias' encounter with Gabriel, the shepherds' annunciation and adoration, and the birth of John the Baptist as the prophesied "messenger" who "shall prepare the way" of the Lord. Luke also relates the Roman census in which "all the world should be taxed" (or registered, enrolled, or counted in versions other than the King James).

Matthew and Luke didn't know each other or each other's work, so far as anyone can tell, and neither witnessed the events in Bethlehem. Yet they agree on some central details. Both report that Joseph had an ancestor in King David and that Mary and Joseph were engaged when an angel told one of them about the coming miraculous conception. Both say the Angel named the unborn child and revealed he would be a savior, or "Christ" by definition of the title that then became a name. Both say these events occurred during Herod's reign, that the birth happened in Bethlehem, and that the family finally settled in Nazareth.

The sharing of these details convinces serious scholars that both Evangelists based their accounts on a body of lore that amounted to common knowledge among the early Christian community. Why wasn't the Nativity recorded earlier? Because it seemed inconsequential. Annunciations aside, the mundane birth of Jesus, an event of extraordinarily commonplace circumstances, held little interest; people were captivated by word of death's miraculous aftermath, the Resurrection. Many early believers considered Jesus to be essentially a man in life until crucifixion brought him immortality.

Luke and Matthew sought to set the record straight so far as their own intimate understanding and convictions were concerned. Luke stressed that Jesus was divine at least from the moment of conception; Matthew that His divinity was prefigured by ancient prophesy. If earlier Gospel accounts of Christ's life, teachings, and death omitted part of the oral record, these last two filled the gaps.

9 Luke describes shepherds abiding in the field on the wintry night of Jesus' birth, but it is known that the herdsmen of Palestine stayed at home with their flocks in winter. Matthew described a miraculous star, and an extraordinary celestial event occurred in those days—but just before the Christian Era began according to conventional reckoning. Both Evangelists say that the Nativity occurred during Herod's reign, yet the infamous King died in 4 B.C. If one thing is certain, it is that Jesus was not born on December 25, anno Domini 1.

The error in years was made by one Dionysius Exiguus, a monk who proposed to end the convention of figuring time from Rome's founding and instead count dates from Christ's birth. The idea took hold, but Dennis the Short lost a few years when backtracking through five centuries of uncertain records. Biblical clues and astronomical data confirm this.

In 4 B.C. Chinese astronomers witnessed a spectacular star, which could also have been seen in Palestine if it was (as modern astronomers suggest) a supernova—the spectacular blaze of light from some sun's explosion in a distant galaxy. Korean chronicles mention the same rare phenomenon, or another one, a year earlier.

If the star of Bethlehem was not a supernova, it could have been the "convergence" of stars or planets into one apparent celestial light. A German astronomer first suggested this three centuries ago and extrapolated the alignment of Mars, Saturn, and Jupiter in the night sky circa 7 B.C. Later calculations have shown that this occurred three times during that year. Be that as it may, most modern authorities conclude that Jesus was born in 5 B.C., plus or minus one.

As for the day of the birth, or of Christ's Mass, Pope Julius I selected December 25 to settle a disagreement between dissonant sects in the fourth century. (Since then almost every other day of the year has been suggested as the actual birth date. A typical line of reasoning held that the Messiah's coming must have commemorated the Creation, which occurred in springtime since Eden was in flower, and therefore .... Be that also as it may.)

The Pope's choice had temporal implications. The date coincided with the most popular Roman festival of the time, the Saturnalia, a period of revelry, feasting, and fertility rites. It also conformed with Hannukah, the Jewish Feast of Lights, and with the birth of Mithras, the new Persian sungod and principal of a growing religion that nearly eclipsed Christianity.

Perhaps most important for Christendom's eventual growth, the date coincided closely with the solstice, a time of singular importance to pre-Christian peoples throughout the northern hemisphere. The Venerable Bede, an early English divine, wrote that "ancient peoples of the Angli began the year on the 25th of December, and the very night which is now so holy to us they called... the mother's night." The Norse celebrated twelve days of Yuletide around the solstice to honor Odin and burned log fires continuously to revive the dying sun.

If the many cultures of the ancient world held one day sacred in common, this was the one, and so Julius could not have made a better choice. The reason why it fell to him as late as the fourth century echoes the absence of Nativity lore in the earliest New Testament writings: The first Christians did not regard the birth of Christ as very special. As the young religion grew more ceremonial, it came to ritually recognize the birth. It only helped the new faith's popularity that this feast happened to fall on a day when much of the northern world was in a holiday mood.

10 Some pagan elements of Christmas gained Christian currency despite the determined wrath of a church militant. But often more politic heads welcomed, or at least permitted, pagan habits.

In England at the turn of the seventh century, Augustine of

Canterbury tended a growing flock who had held the solstice sacred and bedecked their shrines with winter greenery to symbolize the hopeful return of fertility throughout the world. The season was rife with feasting, in part because livestock were slaughtered en masse for want of fodder to feed them until spring. The old shrines were consecrated to the new faith, and native celebrations—holly, ivy, and all—were adapted to Christmas.

Pope Gregory the Great encouraged Augustine in this adroit approach among his people. He wrote the missionary "Nor let them now sacrifice animals to the Devil, but to the praise of God kill animals for their own eating and render thanks to the giver of all their abundance.... For from obdurate minds it is impossible to cut off everything at once."

Indeed, the spirit of the feasting has barely abated in thirteen centuries (despite the Puritan experiment that briefly banned Christmas in England and colonial Massachusetts). As for the greenery, we still deck our halls with holly wreaths and sprays of pine, with mistletoe sprigs, ivy trains, and New World favorites like poinsettia, which comes from Mexico. (Called "flower of the holy night," poinsettia is said to have sprung up miraculously where a pauper knelt to pray on Christmas Eve.) All these trimmings, and their plastic counterfeits, grew from adapted legacies endowed by pagans who were converted—and, in converting, changed Christmas.

11

Matthew profited from hindsight when he explained how events in his Gospel fulfilled what ancient prophets had foretold. These Old Testament visionaries were a peculiar lot who believed themselves—and were perceived to be—possessed of divine wisdom. They invited states of ecstacy, which means to become "'beside oneself,' thrown into a frenzy or stupor, with anxiety, astonishment, fear or passion."

A modern Hebrew scholar writes that these men included "some of the most disturbing people who ever lived.... Instead of showing us a way through the elegant mansion of the mind, the prophets take us to the slums." Typically misanthropic, they shrieked at everything that was immediately wrong with their world and predicted terrible things for errant folk. Yet within their images of doom shone bright figures and well-remembered promises of a Messiah, a divinely anointed one.

Dozens of Old Testament motifs disposed the Jews to expect a savior. The Apostles and early converts believed Jesus was the promised one. The conservative Temple establishment insisted he was not and meant to quash the upstart sect that threatened their lofty status. A determined advocate, Matthew addressed Jewry and appealed to Old Testament authority, the voices of the prophets. After describing Herod's murder of the Innocents, for example, he quotes Jeremiah almost verbatim regarding Rachel's mourning. In Matthew's time such a citation could be regarded as valid argument and must have been powerfully persuasive to people who knew the Old Testament intimately.

If there was no miracle in Matthew's citing prophesy and announcing its fulfillment—he just made certain his audience didn't miss the point—were any prophesies miraculously fulfilled? Perhaps. The Book of Numbers, for instance, described "There shall come a star out of Jacob and a sceptre [or comet] shall rise out of Israel," as one evidently did.

But this bears remembering: There might well be historical or scientific explanations for every so-called miracle, while others may be dismissed as coincidence. Yet a true miracle, by definition, needs no explanation nor has one even if it can be easily explained. Any specific miracle is, again by definition, simply miraculous.

12

The first church of my memory had a very blue rose window, which might be why I could believe —at a young age and even now—that blue roses may grow. Call me hopelessly naive, but consider: However botanically unknown a blue rose may be today, one is not impossible in the horticultural future or the fossil past. Things change. What was may never be again; what will be has never been. Therein lies another lesson learned in childhood: *that* church was transformed once each year.

I was taken there a few ordinary Sundays at most, on sunny mornings because my elders were not the sort to walk through city rain or brave the slush unnecessarily. So the white marble edifice gleamed in the daylight when I saw it, a shining palace among the brownstones and brick apartment blocks. Inside, the stained-glass window scenes flashed down the length of the mock gothic bays. The nave glistened gold and vivid blues and shimmering scarlets from one winter to the next while I sat on an oak pew and swung my legs. Then came the one night of the year when we went religiously, fair weather or foul, just before suppertime to the Children's Service—on Christmas Eve, of course.

The church became a different space in that dark hour when the stories-tall windows stood blank and black, reaching toward the hidden arches of the distant roof. Nothing looked the same among the ribbons and the fir sprays, the lilies and the tinsel-silvered trees. Did all the light come from candles? I cannot remember any more than the breath-blown flames the singers held as they processed in crimson and white linen. Then the play began, in the tradition that St. Francis of Assisi began in 1223 when he had grown people take parts and placed live animals beside the manger.

Two of the "shepherds abiding in the field" of the carpeted crossing lived in my best friend's apartment house. I knew one of the Wise Men from school, and my sister went to dancing class with the girl playing Mary who cradled the swaddled doll with a china face.

Each numinous night there was a carol and a prayer, then "It came to pass that in those days there went out a decree..." and "Silent night, holy night..." and "So it was that while they were there the days were accomplished..." Then, for a moment in the flickering darkness, the girl was in Bethlehem and the babe laughed.

A Christmas Testament

IN THE BEGINNING GOD created the heavens and the earth. Genesis 1
And the earth was without form and void, and darkness was upon the face of the deep, and the Spirit of God moved upon the face of the waters.
And God said 'Let there be light.' And there was light.
God saw the light, that it was good, and God divided the

light from the darkness. And the evening and the morning were the first day.

SO God created man in His own image. In the image of God created He him; male and female created He them. And God blessed them and said unto them 'Be fruitful and multiply and replenish the earth.'

Genesis 2 HE
LORD GOD formed man of the dust of the ground, and breathed into his nostrils the breath of life, and man became a living soul. And the Lord God planted a garden east-ward in Eden and there He put the man whom He had formed. Out of the ground

made the Lord God to grow every tree that is pleasant to the sight and good for food. He set the tree of life also in the midst of the garden and the tree of the knowledge of good and evil. And the Lord God took the man and put him into the Garden of Eden to dress it and keep it.

Genesis 3 NOW THE SERPENT was more subtile than any beast of the field and he said unto the woman 'Yea, hath God said ye shall not eat of every tree of the garden?' And the woman said 'We may eat of the fruit of the trees of the garden. But of the fruit of the tree which is in the midst of the garden God hath said ye

shall not eat of it lest ye die.' And the serpent said 'Ye shall not surely die. For God doth know that in the day ye eat thereof then your eyes shall be opened and ye shall be as gods knowing both good and evil.' And when the woman saw that the tree was good for food and a tree to be desired to make one wise, she took the fruit thereof and did eat. She gave also to her husband with her, and he did eat. And the eyes of them both were opened.

And they heard the voice of the Lord God walking in the garden in the cool of the day and Adam and his wife hid themselves. The Lord God called unto Adam and said

'Where art thou?' The man said 'I heard thy voice and I was afraid because I was naked and I hid myself.' And the Lord God said 'Who told thee that thou wast naked? Hast thou eaten of the tree whereof I commanded thee that thou should not eat?' And the man said 'The woman whom thou gavest to be with me, she gave me of the tree and I did eat.' And the woman said 'The serpent beguiled me and I did eat.'

The Lord God said 'Behold, the man is become one of us to know good and evil.' Now lest he put forth his hand and take also of the tree of life and eat and live forever; the Lord God sent him forth from the Garden of Eden to till the ground from whence he was taken. So he drove out the man.

Genesis 22

AND IT CAME TO PASS that God did tempt Abraham and said unto him 'Take now thy son, thine only son Isaac whom thou lovest, and get thee into the land of Moriah, and offer him there for a burnt offering upon one of the mountains.' Abraham arose up early and saddled his ass. He took the wood of the burnt offering and laid it upon Isaac his son. He took the fire in his hand and a knife and they went both of them together. And Isaac spake unto Abraham and said 'Father, behold the fire and the wood, but where is the lamb for the burnt offering?' And Abraham said 'My son, God will provide Himself a lamb.'

THEY came to the place which God had told him of and Abraham built an altar there and laid the wood in order and bound Isaac his son and laid him on the altar upon the wood.

And Abraham stretched forth his hand and took the knife to slay his son. And the Angel of the Lord called unto him out of heaven and said 'Abraham, Abraham lay not thine hand upon the lad. For now I know that thou fearest God, seeing thou hast not withheld thy son, thine only son, from me.' And Abraham lifted up his eyes and looked and beheld behind him a ram caught in a thicket by his horns. Abraham took the ram and offered it up for a burnt offering in the stead of his son.

And the Angel of the Lord called unto him out of heaven the second time and said

'By myself have I sworn, saith the Lord, for because thou hast done this thing and not withheld thy son, thine only son, I will bless thee. I will multiply thy seed as the stars of the heaven and as the sand which is upon the sea shore. In thy seed shall all the nations of the earth be blessed, because thou hast obeyed my voice.'

HUS Isaiah 42
SAITH GOD the Lord: 'I have
called thee in righteousness
and will hold thine hand and
will keep thee and give thee
as a covenant for all people,
a light for the gentiles.
'Comfort ye, comfort ye Isaiah 40
my people' saith your God.
'Speak ye comfortably to Jerusalem, and cry unto her that

her warfare is accomplished, that her iniquity is pardoned.'

The voice of him that crieth: 'In the wilderness prepare ye the way of the Lord. Make straight in the desert a highway for your God. And the glory of the Lord shall be revealed, and all flesh shall see it together; for the mouth of the Lord hath spoken it.'

Jeremiah 23

Behold the days come,' saith the Lord, 'that I will raise unto David a righteous Branch, and a King shall reign and prosper, and shall execute judgment and justice in the earth. And he shall be called the Lord our Righteousness.'

Numbers 24

I shall see him, but not now. I shall behold him, but not nigh. There shall come a star out of Jacob and a comet shall rise out of Israel. Out of Jacob shall come he that shall have dominion.

Malachi 3

But who may abide the day of his coming? And who shall stand when he appeareth? For he is like a refiner's fire, and he shall purify the sons of Levi and purge them as gold and silver; that they may offer unto the Lord an offering in righteousness. Then will the offering of Judah and Jerusalem be:

pleasing unto the Lord, as in the days of old.

When Israel was a child, then I loved him and called my son out of Egypt. Hosea 11

But thou Bethlehem, though thou be little among the clans of Judah, yet out of thee shall come forth unto me he that is to be ruler of Israel, whose goings forth have been from old, from everlasting. And this man shall be the peace. Micah 5

Psalm 72

The kings of Tarshish
and of the isles shall bring
presents. The kings of Sheba
and Seba shall offer gifts. Yea,
all kings shall fall down before him. To him shall be given
the gold of Sheba. His name
shall endure forever and all
nations shall call him blessed.

Malachi 3

Behold I send you a
messenger and he shall prepare
the way before me. The Lord
whom ye seek shall suddenly
come to his temple, even the
messenger of the covenant,
whom ye delight in. Behold,
he shall come,' saith the Lord
of hosts.

Isaiah 7 HE
LORD HIMSELF shall give you
a sign: Behold a virgin shall
conceive and bear a son, and
shall call his name Immanuel.
Isaiah 9 The people that walked in
darkness have seen a great
light. They that dwell in the
land of the shadow of death,
upon them hath the light
shined. For unto us a child is
born, unto us a son is given.

And the government shall be upon his shoulder: and his name shall be called Wonderful, Counsellor, the mighty God, the Everlasting Father, the Prince of Peace. Of the increase of his government and peace there shall be no end upon the throne of David to order it with justice henceforth even for ever. The zeal of the Lord of hosts will perform this.

And there shall come forth a rod out of the stem of Jesse and a Branch shall grow out of his roots. The spirit of the Lord shall rest upon him, the — Isaiah 11

spirit of wisdom and understanding, the spirit of counsel and might, the spirit of knowledge and of the fear of the Lord. And in that day there shall be a root of Jesse which shall stand for an ensign of the people.

Arise, shine, Isaiah 60
for thy light is come, and the glory of the Lord is risen upon thee. For behold, darkness shall cover the earth, and gross darkness the people. But the Lord shall arise upon thee, and his glory shall be seen upon thee. And the Gentiles shall come to thy light, and kings to the brightness of thy rising.

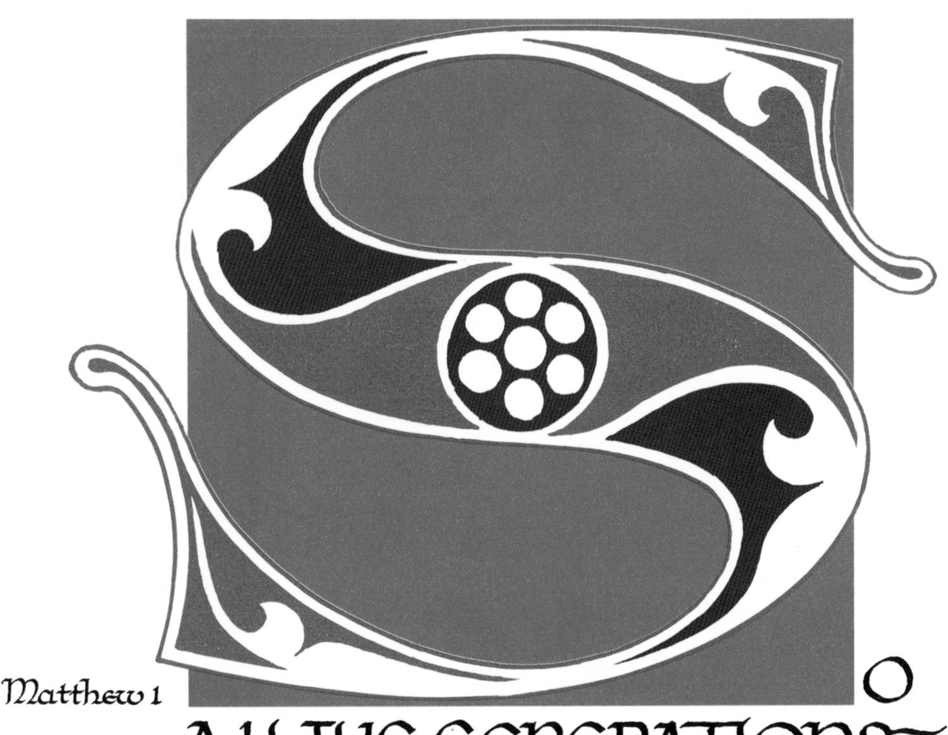

Matthew 1

O ALL THE GENERATIONS
from Abraham to David are
fourteen generations, and
from David until the carrying
away into Babylon are fourteen generations, and from the
carrying away into Babylon
unto Christ are fourteen
generations. Abraham begat
Isaac, and Isaac begat Jacob,
and Jacob begat Judas and

his brethren, and Judas begat Phares and Zara of Thamar; and Phares begat Esrom, and Esrom begat Aram, and Aram begat Aminadab, and Aminadab begat Naasson, and Naasson begat Salmon, and Salmon begat Booz of Rachab, and Booz begat Obed of Ruth, and Obed begat Jesse, and Jesse begat David the King, and David the King begat Solomon of her that had been the wife of Urias the Hittite, and Solomon begat Roboam, and Roboam begat Abia, and Abia begat Asa, and Asa begat Josaphat, and Josaphat begat Joram, and Joram begat Ozias, and Ozias begat Joatham, and Joatham begat Achaz, and Achaz

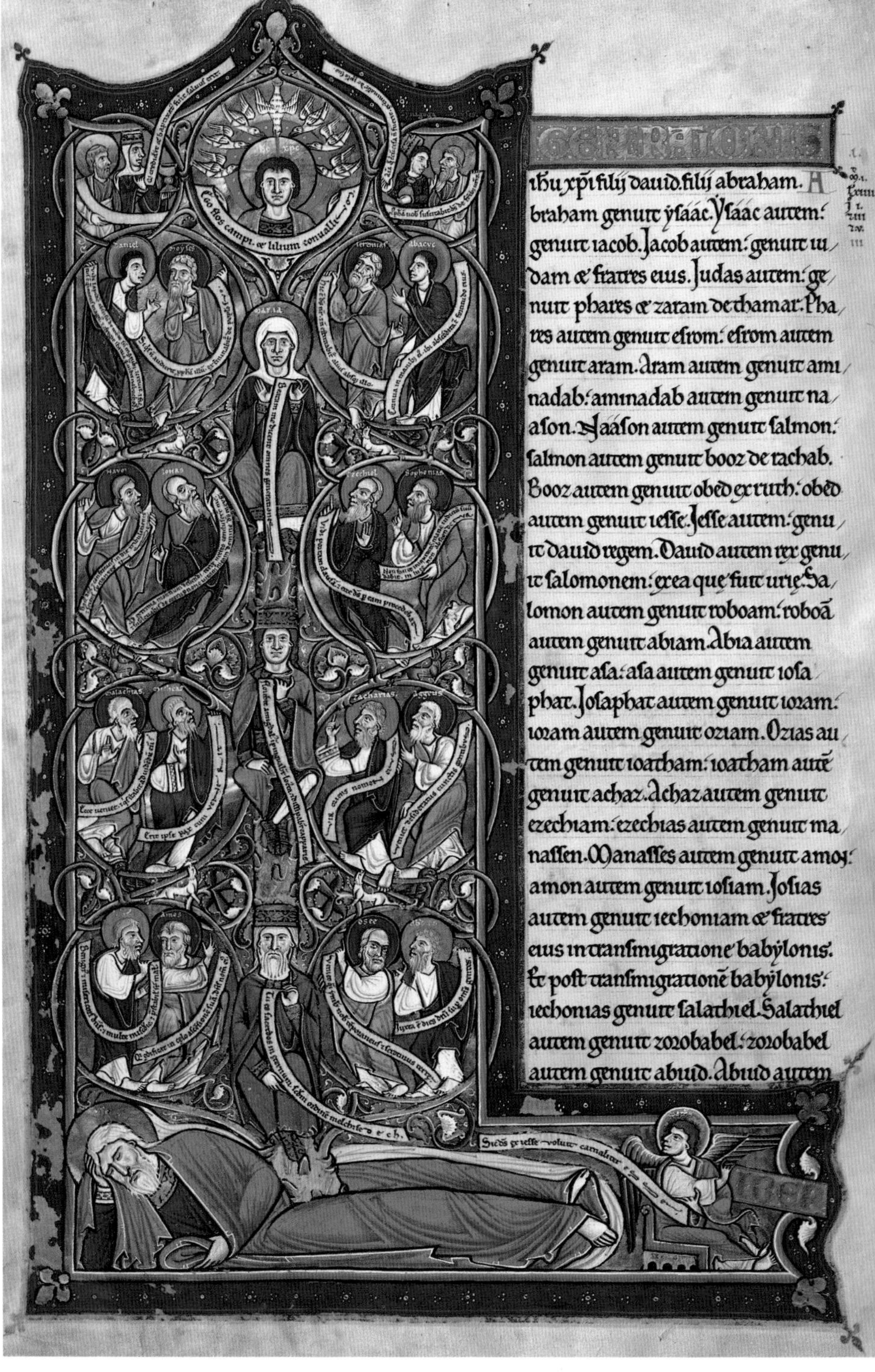

GENERATIONIS

ihu xpi filij dauid. filij abraham. A
braham genuit ysaac. Ysaac autem:
genuit iacob. Jacob autem: genuit iu
dam et fratres eius. Judas autem: ge
nuit phares et zaram de thamar. Pha
res autem genuit esrom: esrom autem
genuit aram. Aram autem genuit ami
nadab: aminadab autem genuit na
ason. Naason autem genuit salmon:
salmon autem genuit booz de rachab.
Booz autem genuit obed ex ruth: obed
autem genuit iesse. Jesse autem: genu
it dauid regem. Dauid autem rex genu
it salomonem: ex ea que fuit urie. Sa
lomon autem genuit roboam: roboā
autem genuit abiam. Abia autem
genuit asa: asa autem genuit iosa
phat. Josaphat autem genuit ioram:
ioram autem genuit oziam. Ozias au
tem genuit ioatham: ioatham autē
genuit achaz. Achaz autem genuit
ezechiam: ezechias autem genuit ma
nassen. Manasses autem genuit amon:
amon autem genuit iosiam. Josias
autem genuit iechoniam et fratres
eius in transmigratione babylonis.
Et post transmigrationē babylonis:
iechonias genuit salathiel. Salathiel
autem genuit zorobabel: zorobabel
autem genuit abiud. Abiud autem

begat Ezekias, and Ezekias
begat Manasses, and Manasses begat Amon, and Amon
begat Josias, and Josias begat
Jaconias and his brethren a-
bout the time they were carried away to Babylon, and after
they were brought to Babylon
Jaconias begat Salathiel, and
Salathiel begat Zorobabel, and
Zorobabel begat Abiud, and A-
biud begat Eliakim, and Eliakim begat Azor; and Azor begat Sadoc, and Sadoc begat
Achim, and Achim begat Eliud,
and Eliud begat Eleazar; and
Eleazar begat Matthan, and
Matthan begat Jacob, and Jacob begat Joseph the husband
of Mary of whom was born
Jesus who is called Christ.

NOW THE BIRTH of Jesus Christ was on this wise: When as his mother Mary was espoused to Joseph, before they came together, she was found with child of the Holy Ghost. Then Joseph, being a just man and not willing to make her a public example, was minded to put her away privily.

But while he thought on these things, behold, the Angel

of the Lord appeared unto him in a dream saying 'Joseph, thou son of David, fear not to take unto thee Mary thy wife, for that which is conceived in her is of the Holy Ghost. She shall bring forth a son and thou shalt call his name Jesus, for he shall save his people from their sins.' Now all this was done that it might be fulfilled which was spoken of the Lord by the prophet saying 'Behold a Virgin shall conceive and bear a son and they shall call his name Emmanuel' which means God with us.

Then Joseph being raised from sleep did as the Angel of the Lord had bidden him, and took unto him his wife and knew her not.

Luke 1 HERE WAS IN THE DAYS of Herod the King of Judea a certain priest named Zacharias of the course of Abia. His wife was of the daughters of Aaron and her name was Elisabeth. They were both righteous before God, walking blameless in all the commandments and ordinances of the Lord. But they had no child because Elisabeth

was barren and they were both now well stricken in years.

And it came to pass according to the custom of the priest's office, his lot was to burn incense when he went into the temple of the Lord. And while the whole multitude of the people were praying without, there appeared unto him an Angel of the Lord standing on the right side of the altar of incense. When Zacharias saw him he was troubled and fear fell upon him. But the Angel said unto him 'Fear not Zacharias, for thy prayer is heard and thy wife Elisabeth shall bear thee a son and thou shalt call his name John. And he shall make ready a people prepared for the Lord.' And

Zacharias said unto the Angel 'Whereby shall I know this? For I am an old man and my wife is well stricken in years.' And the Angel answering said unto him 'I am Gabriel that stand in the presence of God and am sent to speak unto thee and to show thee these glad tidings. And behold thou shalt be dumb and not able to speak until the day that these things shall be performed, because thou believest not my words which shall be fulfilled in their season.'

The people waited for Zacharias and marvelled that he tarried so long in the temple.

And when he came out he could not speak to them and they perceived that he had seen a vision in the temple, for he beckoned unto them and remained speechless. And after those days his wife Elisabeth conceived and hid herself.

ND IN THE SIXTH month the Angel Gabriel was sent from God unto a city in Galilee named Nazareth to a virgin espoused to a man whose name was Joseph of the house of David. And the virgin's name was Mary. The Angel came in unto her and said… 'Hail, thou that art highly favored, the Lord is with thee.

Blessed art thou among women.

When she saw him she was troubled at his saying and cast in her mind what manner of salutation this could be.

And the Angel said unto her 'Fear not Mary, for thou hast found favor with God. And behold, thou shalt conceive in thy womb and bring forth a son and shalt call his name Jesus. He shall be great and shall be called the Son of the Highest, and the Lord God shall give unto him the throne of his father David. And he shall reign over the house of Jacob for ever and of his king-

dom there shall be no end.'

Then Mary said unto the Angel, 'How shall this be, seeing I know not a man?' And the Angel answered 'The Holy Ghost shall come upon thee and the power of the highest shall overshadow thee. Therefore that holy thing which shall be born of thee shall be

called the Son of God. Behold thy cousin Elisabeth, she hath also conceived a son in her old age and this is the sixth month with her who was called barren. For with God nothing shall be impossible.' And Mary said 'Behold the handmaid of the Lord. Be it unto me according to thy word.'

HE ANGEL DEPARTED from her and Mary arose and went into the hill country with haste into a city of Judah and entered into the house of Zacharias and saluted Elisabeth. When Elisabeth heard the salutation of Mary, the babe leaped in her womb and Elisabeth was filled with the

Holy Ghost. She spake out with a loud voice and said 'Blessed art thou among women and blessed is the fruit of thy womb.' And Mary said 'My soul doth magnify the Lord, and my spirit hath rejoiced in God my savior, For behold from henceforth all generations shall call me blessed, for He that is mighty hath done to me great things and holy is His name.' And Mary abode with Elisabeth about three months.

Now Elisabeth's full time came that she should be delivered and she brought

forth a son. Her neighbors and her cousins heard how the Lord had showed great mercy upon her and they rejoiced and they made signs to his father how he would have him called. He asked for a writing table and wrote, saying 'His name is John.' And his mouth was opened immediately and his tongue was loosed and he spake and praised God.

Zacharias was filled with the

Holy Ghost and prophesied saying 'Blessed be the Lord God of Israel, for He hath visited and redeemed His people, as He spake by the mouth of His holy prophets which have been since the world began. Remember His holy covenant, the oath which He sware to our father Abraham. And thou, child, shalt go before the face of the Lord to prepare His ways.'

T CAME Luke 2

TO PASS in those days that there went out a decree from Caesar Augustus that all the world should be taxed. And all went to be enrolled, every one into his own city. Joseph also went up from Galilee, out of the city of Nazareth into Judea unto the city of David which is called Bethlehem, to be taxed with Mary his espoused wife, being great with child.

O IT WAS that while they were there the days were accomplished that she should be delivered.

And she brought forth her firstborn son and wrapped him in swaddling clothes and laid him in a manger, because there was no room for them in the inn.

ND THERE WERE in the same country shepherds abiding in the field, keeping watch over their flock by night. And lo, the Angel of the Lord came upon them, and the glory of the Lord shone round about them, and they were sore afraid. And the Angel said unto them 'Fear not, for behold I bring you good tidings of great joy which shall be to all people. For unto you is born this day

in the city of David a Savior
which is Christ the Lord. And
this shall be a sign unto you:
Ye shall find the babe wrapped
in swaddling clothes, lying in a

manger.' And suddenly there
was with the Angel a multitude of the heavenly host prais-

ing God and saying 'Glory to God in the highest, and on earth peace, good will toward men.'

ADORAMVS TE GLORIFICAM
ADORAMVS TE GLORIF
ADORAMVS TE GL

AND IT CAME TO PASS as the Angels were gone away from them into heaven, the shepherds said one to another, 'Let us now go even unto Bethlehem and

see this thing which is come to
pass, which the Lord hath made
known unto us.' They came with

haste and found Mary and Joseph, and the babe lying in a manger.

ND WHEN THEY HAD seen it they made known abroad the saying which was told them concerning this child. And all they that heard it wondered at those things which were told them by the shepherds. But Mary kept all those things and pondered them in her heart. And the shepherds returned, glorifying and praising God for all the things that they had heard and seen. And when eight days were accomplished for the circumcising of the child, his name was called Jesus, which was so named by the Angel before he was conceived in the womb.

When the days of her purification according to the Law of Moses were accomplished, they brought him to Jerusalem to present him to the Lord. And behold, there was a man in Jerusalem whose name was Simeon, and the same man was just and devout, waiting for the restoration of Israel. And it was revealed to him by the Holy Ghost that he should not see death before he had seen the Lord's Christ.

IOANNES

And he came by the Spirit into the temple, and when the parents brought in the child Jesus, he took Him up in his arms and blessed God, and said: 'Lord, now lettest thou thy servant depart in peace according to thy word. For mine eyes have seen thy salvation, which thou hast prepared before the face of all people, a light to enlighten the Gentiles, and the glory of thy people Israel.' And Joseph and His mother marvelled at those things.

Matthew 2

OW
WHEN JESUS was born
in Bethlehem of Judea in the
days of Herod the king, behold,
there came wise men from the
east to Jerusalem saying —
'Where is He that is born
King of the Jews? For we
have seen His star rising in the
east and are come to worship
Him.'

When Herod heard
these things he was troubled,

+HERODES REGES MAGI

and all Jerusalem with him. When he had gathered all the chief priests and scribes of the people together, he demanded of them where Christ should be born. And they said unto him, 'In Bethlehem, for thus it is written by the prophet: Thou Bethlehem art not the least among the princes of Judah, for out of thee shall come a governor that shall rule my people Israel.'

HEN HEROD, when he had privily called the wise men, inquired of them what time the star appeared. And he sent them to Bethlehem and said 'Go and search diligently for the young child. And when ye have found Him bring me word again that I may come and worship Him also.'

When they heard the King they departed. And lo,

the star which they saw in the east went before them till it came and stood over the place where the young child lay.

And when they were come into the house they saw the young child with Mary His mother and fell down and worshipped Him. When they had opened their treasures, they presented unto Him gifts: gold, frankincense and myrrh. And being warned

of God in a dream that they should not return to Herod, —they departed to their own country another way.

REGES TARSIS 7 INSVLE MVNERA OFFERET REGES ARABV 7 SABBA DONA ADVCET. PS. LXXI. C
ET APERTIS THESAVRIS SVIS OBTVLERVT EI AVRVM THVS 7 MIRRAM. MACTI. I. C.

HEN THEY WERE departed, behold, the Angel of the Lord appeared to Joseph in a dream saying 'Arise and take the young child and His mother and flee into Egypt. Be thou there until I bring thee word, for Herod will seek the young child to destroy Him.'

When he arose he took the young child and His mother by night and departed into Egypt and was there

until the death of Herod, that it might be fulfilled which was spoken of the Lord by the prophet, saying 'Out of Egypt have I called my son.'

DIXIT Dominus domino psal'
meo: ſede a dextris meis
Donec ponam inimicos
os: ſcabellum pedum tuorum

HEN HEROD, when he saw that he was mocked by the wise men, was exceeding wroth and sent forth and slew all the children that were in Bethlehem from two years old and under, according to the time which he had diligently inquired of the wise men. Then was fulfilled that which

was spoken by the prophet saying 'In Rama was there a voice heard, lamentation and weeping and great mourning, Rachel weeping for her children and would not be comforted, because they were not.'

UT WHEN Herod was dead, behold, an Angel of the Lord appeared in a dream to Joseph in Egypt saying 'Arise and take the young child and His mother and go into the land of Israel, for they are dead which sought the young child's life.

He arose and took the young child and His mother and came into the land of Israel. Being

warned of God in a dream, he turned aside into the parts of Galilee. He came and dwelt in a city called Nazar-

eth that it might be fulfilled which was spoken by the prophets: 'He shall be called a Nazarene.'

IN THE BEGINNING was the Word, and the Word was with God and the Word was God. All things were made by Him and without Him was not anything made that was made. In Him was life and the life was the light of men. And the light shineth in darkness and the darkness comprehended it not.

John 1

He was in the world, and the world was made by Him and the world knew Him not. He came unto His own and His own received Him not. But as many as received Him, to them gave He power to become the sons of God, even to them that believe in His name, which were born not of blood nor of the will of the flesh nor of the will of man but of God.

And the Word was made flesh and dwelt among us. And we beheld His glory, the glory as of the only begotten of the Father, full of grace and truth.

with thanks

I am especially grateful to the Rev. Jo C. Tartt, Jr. As rector of Grace Episcopal Church in Washington, D.C., he offered me the opportunity to compose the Christmas service which evolved into this book. Those who joined in the original program and gave life to the words also deserve warm thanks: Patricia Gordon-Cumming, Austin P. Frum, Thomas P. McCarley, Terence Roche Murphy, Alan Osbourne and Laura Wheelock.

Once my wife and I embarked on compiling *A Christmas Testament,* we encountered friends and strangers who provided vital help. We thank them all:

Dr. Arthur K. Wheelock, Jr., curator of Dutch and Flemish Painting at the National Gallery of Art (and Laura's father), offered both early encouragement and sound advice about art history.

Executive librarians Caroline Backlund and Lamia Doumato made the National Gallery's invaluable bibliographic resources available to us. This rich repository was our prime source in locating the world's masterpieces of Nativity art.

Dr. Theodore Feder, president of Editorial Photocolor Archives, Inc., and his colleague Cindy Trueman, later put their matchless collection of photographs at our disposal and provided us with transparencies unavailable elsewhere.

Kathleen Hunt, librarian of the Rosenwald Collection at the Library of Congress, located manuscripts and Books of Hours, and facilitated their reproduction.

The Rev. Dr. Arthur R. McKay, minister of Washington's New York Avenue Presbyterian Church, and Merrill Ware Carrington, M. Div., introduced me to biblical scholarship.

Ruth Felter typed innumerable lists of art works as we pursued the selection process.

Our publishers enlisted two key people to work literally on the words: consulting editor Evelyn Bence brought the leaven of special knowledge to bear in reviewing the texts; and, rendering the Bible selections on paper, Polly Johnson dedicated her calligraphic gifts to the book. We thank them both, along with co-editor-in-chief Susan E. Meyer who handled logistics and editing with deft skill.

For artistic guidance—and much more—we are indebted to co-publisher Nai Chang who worked closely with us in selecting a group of paintings from several hundred possibilities. He then conceived the graphic book and played an active central role while his wife, designer Wei-Wen Chang, carried the design to fruition.

Finally, the reader must know that *A Christmas Testament* sees the light of publication because of one man, Andrew Stewart, its publisher, who believed in this project from the start. For his many personal gifts—including integrity and vision—we will remember him with thanks each Christmas.

PICTURE CREDITS

Slipcase, detail from *Flight into Egypt* by Giotto. Basilica of St. Francis, Assisi. Photograph: Scala/Editorial Photocolor Archives, New York.

Page 1, *Madonna and Child* by Gentile da Fabriano. National Gallery of Art, Washington; Samuel H. Kress Collection.

Page 12, untitled painting by Fra Angelico from the door of a chest. San Marco, Florence. Photograph: Scala/Editorial Photocolor Archives, New York.

Page 26, *Madonna and Child with the Baptist and Saint Peter* attributed to Giovanni Cimabue. National Gallery of Art, Washington; Samuel H. Kress Collection.

Page 27, detail from *Creation of the Stars and Planets* by Michelangelo. Sistine Chapel, Vatican, Rome. Photograph: Scala/Editorial Photocolor Archives, New York.

Page 29, left panel from *Garden of Eden* triptych by Hieronymus Bosch. Copyright© Prado Museum, Madrid.

Pages 30–31, *Adam and Eve in Paradise* by Lucas Cranach. Scala/Editorial Photocolor Archives, New York.

Page 32, detail from *Adam and Eve in Paradise* by Lucas Cranach. Scala/Editorial Photocolor Archives, New York.

Page 34, detail from *Adam and Eve in Paradise* by Lucas Cranach. Scala/Editorial Photocolor Archives, New York.

Page 35, *Eve Tempted by the Serpent* by Lucas Cranach the Elder, circa 1530. The Art Institute of Chicago; Charles H. and Mary F. S. Worcester Collection. Photograph: Joseph Martin/Scala/Editorial Photocolor Archives, New York.

Page 37, detail from *Adam and Eve in Paradise* by Lucas Cranach. Scala/Editorial Photocolor Archives, New York.

Pages 38–39, *The Garden of Eden* by Erastus Salisbury Field, painted circa 1860–70. Courtesy Museum of Fine Arts, Boston; M. and M. Karolik Collection.

Page 41, *Expulsion* by Tommaso Masaccio. Brancacci Chapel, Florence. Photograph: Scala/Editorial Photocolor Archives, New York.

Page 42, detail from *The Sacrifice of Isaac* by Giovanni Domenico Tiepolo. The Metropolitan Museum of Art (Purchase 1871).

Page 45, *Sacrifice of Isaac* by Rembrandt van Rijn. The Hermitage, Leningrad.

Page 46, *The Sacrifice of Isaac*, 5th century mosaic. San Vitale, Ravenna. Photograph: Scala/Editorial Photocolor Archives, New York.

Page 49, left panel, the Prophet Isaiah, from *Nativity with the Prophets Isaiah and Ezekiel* by Duccio di Buoninsegna. National Gallery of Art, Washington; Andrew W. Mellon Collection.

Page 53, right panel, the Prophet Ezekiel, from *Nativity with the Prophets Isaiah and Ezekiel* by Duccio di Buoninsegna. National Gallery of Art, Washington; Andrew W. Mellon Collection.

Page 54, detail from *The Alba Madonna* by Raphael. National Gallery of Art, Washington; Andrew W. Mellon Collection.

Page 56, *Tree of Jesse*. Cathedral of Autun, St. Lazare. Photograph: Scala/Editorial Photocolor Archives, New York.

Page 60, *The Jesse Tree* from the Bible of Saint-Bertin. Bibliothèque Nationale, Paris.

Page 62, detail from *The Nativity with the Infant Saint John* by Piero di Cosimo. National Gallery of Art, Washington; Samuel H. Kress Collection.

Pages 66–67, *The Angel with Zacharias* by Berner Nelkenmeister. Kunstmuseum, Bern.

Page 69, detail from *The Annunciation* by Giovanni di Paolo. National Gallery of Art, Washington; Samuel H. Kress Collection.

Pages 70–71, *Annunciation* by Leonardo da Vinci. Uffizi, Florence. Photograph: Scala/Editorial Photocolor Archives, New York.

Pages 72–73, *Annunciation* by Giovanni di Paolo. National Gallery of Art, Washington; Samuel H. Kress Collection.

Pages 74–75, *Annunciation* by Fra Angelico, 1455. Copyright© Prado Museum, Madrid.

Page 76, *The Annunciation* by Fra Filippo Lippi. National Gallery of Art, Washington; Samuel H. Kress Collection.

Page 77, *Annunciation*. Bourges. Photograph: Scala/Editorial Photocolor Archives, New York.

Pages 78–79, details from *The Annunciation* by Pietro Perugino. National Gallery of Art, Washington; Samuel H. Kress Collection.

Page 80, detail from *Annunciation* by Fra Angelico. Copyright© Prado Museum, Madrid.

Page 81, *Visitation* by Rueland Frueauf the Elder, circa 1495. Courtesy Busch-Reisinger Museum, Harvard University, Cambridge.

Pages 82–83, *The Visitation with Saint Nicholas and Saint Anthony Abbot* by Piero di Cosimo. National Gallery of Art, Washington; Samuel H. Kress Collection.

Page 85, *Maria and Elisabeth*. Chartres. Photograph: Scala/Editorial Photocolor Archives, New York.

Page 87, detail from *The Virgin and St. Joseph Arriving at the Inn in Bethlehem* by Cornelis Massys. Berlin-Dahlem, Staatliche Museen. Photograph: Jörg P. Anders.

Pages 88–89, *Census of Bethlehem* by Pieter Brueghel. Museum of Ancient Art, Brussels. Photograph: Scala/Editorial Photocolor Archives, New York.

Page 91, *Nativity* by Fra Angelico. San Marco, Florence. Photograph: Scala/Editorial Photocolor Archives, New York.

Page 92, center panel from *Nativity with the Prophets Isaiah and Ezekiel* by Duccio di Buoninsegna. National Gallery of Art, Washington; Andrew W. Mellon Collection.

Page 93, detail from a painting by Fra Angelico on the door of a chest. San Marco, Florence. Photograph: Scala/Editorial Photocolor Archives, New York.

Pages 94–95, *Nativity* by Giotto. Basilica of St. Francis, Assisi. Photograph: Scala/Editorial Photocolor Archives, New York.

Page 96, *Nativity* by Giotto. Scrovegni Chapel, Padua. Photograph: Scala/Editorial Photocolor Archives, New York.

Page 97, *The Nativity* by Petrus Christus. National Gallery, Washington; Andrew W. Mellon Collection.

Pages 98–99, *The Nativity* by Fra Filippo Lippi and Assistant. National Gallery of Art, Washington; Samuel H. Kress Collection.

Page 100, detail from *Angels in Adoration* by Benozzo Gozzoli. Palazzo Medici-Riccardi, Florence. Photograph: Scala/Editorial Photocolor Archives, New York.

Page 101, detail from *Angels in Adoration* by Benozzo Gozzoli. Palazzo Medici-Riccardi, Florence. Photograph: Scala/Editorial Photocolor Archives, New York.

Page 102, *The Annunciation to the Shepherds* by Jacopo Bassano. National Gallery of Art, Washington; Samuel H. Kress Collection.

Page 103, top, detail from *The Adoration of the Shepherds* by Giovanni Girolamo Savoldo. National Gallery of Art, Washington; Samuel H. Kress Collection.

Page 103, bottom, *Adoration of the Magi* from a predella by Gentile da Fabriano. Uffizi, Florence. Photograph: Scala/Editorial Photocolor Archives, New York.

Pages 104–105, *Adoration of the Shepherds* by Hugo van der Goes. Berlin-Dahlem, Staatliche Museen. Photograph: Jörg P. Anders.

Pages 106–107, *The Adoration of the Shepherds* by Giorgione. National Gallery of Art, Washington; Samuel H. Kress Collection.

Page 108, *Virgin and Child* by Rogier van der Weyden. Musée des Beaux-Arts, Caen.

Page 109, detail from *Madonna and Child in a Landscape* by Giovanni Bellini. National Gallery of Art, Washington; Ralph and Mary Booth Collection.

Page 111, *Madonna and Child with Saints* by Giovanni Bellini. National Gallery of Art, Washington; Samuel H. Kress Collection.

Page 112, detail from *Nativity*. Duomo, Trento. Photograph: Scala/Editorial Photocolor Archives, New York.

Page 114, detail from *Saint Matthew and Angel Gabriel* by Rembrandt van Rijn, 1661. Musée du Louvre; Cliché Musées Nationaux, Paris.

Page 115, top, *Magi Led by the Star*. Canterbury Cathedral. Photograph: Manu Sassoonian/Scala/Editorial Photocolor Archives, New York.

Page 115, bottom, *Magi Consulting with Herod*, 13th century. Canterbury Cathedral. Photograph: Manu Sassoonian/Scala/Editorial Photocolor Archives, New York.

Page 116, detail from *The Three Kings*. Basilica of St. Apollinare Nuovo, Ravenna. Photograph: Scala/Editorial Photocolor Archives, New York.

Page 117, detail from *Adoration of the Magi*. Staufberg. Scala/Editorial Photocolor Archives, New York.

Page 118, *Adoration of the Magi* by Hugo van der Goes. Berlin-Dahlem, Staatliche Museen. Photograph: Jörg P. Anders.

Page 119, *The Adoration of the Magi* by Benvenuto di Giovanni. National Gallery of Art, Washington; Andrew W. Mellon Collection.

Pages 120–121, *Adoration of the Magi* by Rogier van der Weyden. Alte Pinakothek, Munich. Photograph: Scala/Editorial Photocolor Archives, New York.

Page 122, top, detail from a painting by Fra Angelico on the door of a chest. San Marco, Florence. Photograph: Scala/Editorial Photocolor Archives, New York.

Pages 122–123, top, *The Adoration of the Magi* by Sandro Botticelli. National Gallery of Art, Washington; Andrew W. Mellon Collection.

Pages 122–123, bottom, *Adoration of the Magi*, tapestry from Musée des Tissus, Lyon. Photograph: Scala/Editorial Photocolor Archives, New York.

Page 124, top, detail from a painting by Fra Angelico on the door of a chest. San Marco, Florence. Photograph: Scala/ Editorial Photocolor Archives, New York.

Page 124, bottom, border detail from *Flight into Egypt* by Giotto. Basilica of St. Francis, Assisi. Photograph: Scala/Editorial Photocolor Archives, New York.

Page 125, top, border detail from *Flight into Egypt* by Giotto. Basilica of St. Francis, Assisi. Photograph: Scala/Editorial Photocolor Archives, New York.

Page 125, bottom, *Dream of Joseph* by Giotto. Scrovegni Chapel, Padua. Photograph: Scala/Editorial Photocolor Archives, New York.

Page 126, *Flight into Egypt* by Giotto. Scrovegni Chapel, Padua. Photograph: Scala/Editorial Photocolor Archives, New York.

Page 127, *Flight into Egypt* by Giotto. Basilica of St. Francis, Assisi. Photograph: Scala/Editorial Photocolor Archives, New York.

Page 128, *The Rest on the Flight into Egypt* by Quentin Massys, 16th century. Worcester Art Museum, Worcester, Massachusetts.

Page 129, *The Flight Into Egypt* from the Flemish *Horae Beatae Mariae*, 15th century. The Lessing J. Rosenwald Collection, Library of Congress, Washington, D.C.

Page 130, detail from *The Visitation with Saint Nicholas and Saint Anthony Abbot* by Piero di Cosimo. National Gallery of Art, Washington; Samuel H. Kress Collection.

Page 131, *Massacre of the Innocents* by Giotto. Scrovegni Chapel, Padua. Photograph: Scala/Editorial Photocolor Archives, New York.

Page 133, *The Rest on the Flight into Egypt* by Gerard David. National Gallery of Art, Washington; Andrew W. Mellon Collection.

Pages 134–135, *The Flight into Egypt* by Vittore Carpaccio. National Gallery of Art, Washington; Andrew W. Mellon Collection.

Page 136, *The Annunciation* by Paolo Veronese. National Gallery of Art, Washington; Samuel H. Kress Collection.

Page 137, detail from *The Annunciation* by Paolo Veronese. National Gallery of Art, Washington; Samuel H. Kress Collection.

Page 139, *The Coronation of the Virgin* by Agnolo Gaddi. National Gallery of Art, Washington; Samuel H. Kress Collection.

Typography in Trump Medieval Medium by U.S. Lithograph Inc., New York, New York.

Printing in five-color offset on 157 gsm matte-coated paper by Toppan Printing Company, Ltd., Tokyo, Japan.

Bound in Japan by Toppan Printing Company, Ltd.